The Customary International Law of Cyberspace

The first thing to know about international law is that it bears only a passing resemblance to the kind of law with which most people are familiar. Domestic laws in most countries are passed by some sort of sovereign body (like Congress) after due consideration. Statutes are carefully crafted so the law has a precise effect. International law is nothing like that. Contrary to popular belief, treaties are not the primary means of establishing international law. The body of international law is a jumble of historic practice and tradition as well as signed agreements between nations.

Within this patchwork of guidance, customary international law occupies a position of preeminence in developing areas of the law—ahead of treaties and conventions.[1] Customary international law develops from the general and consistent practice of states if the practice is followed out of a sense of legal obligation.[2] When this occurs, customary law is considered legally binding on nation-states. In situations not addressed by established consensus on what constitutes lawful behavior, nations may take actions they deem appropriate.[3] This is the heart of the well-established *Lotus* principle, so named for the International Court of Justice decision in which it was established.[4]

Only a handful of actions are considered peremptory norms of international law; that is, things that are universally held to be wrong and impermissible.[5] These are exceptional areas, including piracy, human trafficking, and hijacking. One reason there are so few universally accepted norms is the very nature of the international legal regime. It is established

Col Gary Brown has been the staff judge advocate (SJA) at US Cyber Command, Fort Meade, Maryland, since its establishment in 2010. Previously, he was the SJA at Joint Functional Component Command—Network Warfare. He is a graduate of the University of Nebraska College of Law.

Maj Keira Poellet is an operations law attorney at US Cyber Command. Her previous assignment was deputy SJA at Lajes Field, Azores, Portugal. She received her LLM in space and telecommunications law from the University of Nebraska College of Law and her JD from Whittier Law School.

by what nations do and believe they are bound to do, making consensus difficult to reach. Without consensus, there is no law, even in what seem to be straightforward cases, such as torture. "Torture or cruel, inhuman, or degrading treatment or punishment" is recognized by most states as violating human rights principles that have attained the status of customary international law. Yet, actions amounting to torture continue, and states sponsoring those actions are not often condemned, so it cannot be said there is complete international agreement on the issue.[6]

Although the few prohibitions accepted as peremptory norms do not deal with war, that is not to say armed conflict is completely ungoverned. There is a body of customary law reflecting the extensive and virtually uniform conduct of nation-states during traditional warfare that is widely accepted and well understood—the law of war. Unfortunately, the application of the law of war to cyberspace is problematic because the actions and effects available to nations and nonstate actors in cyberspace do not necessarily match up neatly with the principles governing armed conflict. Cyberspace gives nation-states new options, enabling them to take non-kinetic actions that may not have been available previously. Actions that may have required the use of military force in previous conflicts now can be done with cyber techniques without the use of force. States can also take actions in cyberspace that would be consistent with the use of armed force but more easily avoid taking responsibility for the actions—they can take cyber action "without attribution."

In the absence of a specific legal regime for cyberspace, the logical approach is to take what guidance exists to govern more conventional warfare and determine whether it can be applied to cyberspace activities. The subsequent brief discussion is a general examination of how national practices become customs binding on the body of nations as customary international law. Following the general discussion is a more detailed discussion of how customary international law might apply to nation-state cyber actions.

The Development of Customary International Law

It is common for states to disagree about what constitutes a general practice accepted as law. The easiest form of proof is found in state actions, published government materials, official government statements, domestic laws, and court decisions that detail actual practice.[7] Over time, specific instances of state practice may develop into a general custom.[8]

The second part of the equation is more difficult. For a custom to be binding, states not only need to act in a certain way; they have to act that way because they think they are legally obligated to do so.[9] Acceptance of general practice as an obligation, that it is "accepted by law," is referred to as *opinio juris*.[10] Evidence of *opinio juris* is primarily shown through statements of belief, as opposed to statements about state practice, such as treaties or declarations.[11]

There is no mathematical formula governing how many states must accept a practice or for how long it needs to be practiced for it to become binding custom.[12] For the most part, the more states that practice a custom, the more likely it is to evolve into law, but not even that simple rule holds completely true. The practice of politically powerful and active states carries more weight than that of smaller nations, especially ones not actively engaged in the area under consideration. For example, actions of the United States or Great Britain will have more bearing on the development of international law governing naval operations than those of Switzerland.

As noted, the length of time to develop customary international law can vary greatly. The law of war is a good example. The customary law of war has developed over thousands of years, but the practice of limiting conflict (e.g., to protect noncombatants) evolved primarily in the last 150 years. For example, the Greeks began developing the concept of *jus ad bellum*, or just war, in the fourth century BC.[13] By contrast, while the principles governing the way in which combatants engage in warfare (*jus in bello*) also have historical ties to that era, they did not begin to assume their current form until the 1860s during the Franco-Prussian War and the American Civil War. Documented atrocities during those wars led to rapid development of the modern law of war regime, beginning with the first Hague Convention in 1899.

An example of customary law that developed quickly is space law.[14] In 1958, just one year after the launch of *Sputnik*, the UN General Assembly created a committee to settle on the peaceful uses of outer space. By 1963, the United Nations had put forth the *Declaration of Legal Principles Governing the Activities of States in the Exploration and Use of Outer Space*, formally recognizing what had become customary law applicable to space activities. Since then, most space law has been generated through international agreements, beginning with the first outer space treaty signed in 1967.

Sometimes even state *inaction* can establish practice. For example, when one state engages in conduct harmful to another, the official silence of the "victim" state can be evidence that the conduct in question does not constitute a violation of international law. This passiveness and inaction can produce a binding effect under what is called the doctrine of acquiescence.[15] The more times a state permits an action to occur without meaningful protest, the more likely it is the action will be accepted as lawful state practice.

Development of Cyber Law through Custom

The increasing use of computers and computer networks through the 1970s and 1980s was followed swiftly by the rise of the "network of networks" known as the Internet in the mid-1990s.[16] Ultimately, the Internet spawned an entirely new domain of operations referred to as *cyberspace*. It is in and through this virtual space that cyber activities occur. So, not only are the activities in cyber new, *where* cyber actions take place is a unique location.[17]

Because it has existed for such a short time, there is not a robust body of law governing state conduct in cyberspace.[18] There are documented instances of state cyber practice, however, and these have begun to lay a pattern for establishing customary cyber law. As noted above, customary law does not instantly appear but is developed through state practice and rationale. The cyber practices of states and the thought behind those actions over the past 30 years must be examined to determine if there is customary law in cyberspace. If no principles have developed, as earlier discussed, cyberspace remains unconstrained under the default customary international regime.

Although *opinio juris* is a critical element, it is easiest to analyze the development of custom beginning with an examination of state action, which is more visible and easily documented than motivation. Complicating the analysis is the secrecy surrounding most cyber operations. The US Department of Defense (DoD), for example, claims it suffers millions of scans and thousands of probes into its networks each day.[19] With rare exceptions, no states or individuals come forward to take credit for these actions, so assessing the motivation of these unknown cyber actors is difficult. Albeit complicated and difficult, a few examples of state practice in cyber are available for examination.

Arguably, the first cyber attack occurred in the Soviet Union. In 1982, a trans-Siberian pipeline exploded. The explosion was recorded by US satellites, and it was referred to by one US official as "the most monumental nonnuclear explosion and fire ever seen from space."[20] It has been reported the explosion was caused by computer malware the Central Intelligence Agency implanted in Canadian software, apparently knowing the software would be illegally acquired by Soviet agents. Because the explosion happened in remote Siberia, it resulted in no casualties. It also embarrassed the Russian Committee for State Security (the KGB), who thought they had stolen the most recent software technology from the United States. As a result, the facts behind the explosion were concealed, and the USSR never publicly accused the United States of causing the incident.[21]

Multiple "soft" computer attacks occurred against US systems as the Internet grew exponentially over the next 25 years. Many of these involved attempts to copy sensitive information or relatively simple but potentially devastating denial of service attacks.[22] Some of the more infamous include Moonlight Maze (1998–2001), which probed government and academic computer systems in the United States; Code Red (2001), which launched a worm intended to conduct a denial of service attack against White House computers; and Mountain View (2001), a number of intrusions into US municipal computer systems to collect information on utilities, government offices, and emergency systems.[23] Although there was speculation about the origins, none of these incidents could be definitively attributed to a state actor.

In contrast to the, until recently, little-known Siberian incident, it was a very public series of cyber events considered by many to have heralded the advent of cyber warfare. In April 2007, following the removal of a Russian statue in Estonia's capital of Tallinn, a widespread denial of service attack affected its websites. As a result Estonia, one of the world's most wired countries, was forced to cut off international Internet access. Russia denied involvement in the incident, but experts speculate the Russian Federal Security Service (FSB) was behind the distributed denial of service event.[24]

The following year, Russian troops invaded the Republic of Georgia during a dispute over territory in South Ossetia. In August 2008, prior to Russian forces crossing the border, Georgian government websites were subjected to denial of service attacks and defacement. While there is widespread belief the incident was "coordinated and instructed" by elements of the Russian government, no one has been able to attribute these actions definitively to Russia.[25]

The wakeup call for the US military occurred in 2008, although the details did not become public until two years later. Operation Buckshot Yankee was the DoD's response to a computer worm known as "agent.btz" infiltrating the US military's classified computer networks.[26] The worm was placed on a flash drive by a foreign intelligence agency, from where it ultimately made its way to a classified network. The purpose of the malware was to transfer sensitive US defense information to foreign computer servers.[27] In what qualifies as bureaucratic lightning speed, US Cyber Command was established less than two years later, with a mission to, among other things, direct the operations and defense of DoD computer networks.[28] In addition to unmasking the extent of network vulnerabilities, the event highlighted the lack of clarity in international law as it relates to cyber events.

Two recent incidents merit attention before discussing the law in depth. In 2010, Google reported Chinese hackers had infiltrated its systems and stolen intellectual property. Through its investigation, Google learned the exfiltration of its information was not the only nefarious activity; at least 20 other companies had been targeted by Chinese hackers as well. These companies covered a wide range of Google users, including the computer, finance, media, and chemical sectors. The Chinese had also attempted to hack into G-mail accounts of human rights activists and were successful in accessing some accounts through malware and phishing scams. Google released a statement explaining what it discovered through its investigation and what steps it was taking in response to China's action, including limiting its business in and with China.[29]

Also in 2010, a computer worm named Stuxnet was detected on computer systems worldwide. Stuxnet resided on and replicated from computers using Microsoft's Windows operating system but targeted a supervisory control and data acquisition (SCADA) system manufactured by Siemens. Cyber experts determined the worm was designed to affect the automated processes of industrial control systems and speculated that either Iran's Bushehr nuclear power plant or its uranium enrichment facility at Natanz was the intended target.[30] After Stuxnet became public, Iran issued a statement that the delay in the Bushehr plant becoming operational was based on "technical reasons" but did not indicate it was because of Stuxnet.[31] The deputy director of the Atomic Energy Organization of Iran stated,

"Most of the claims made by [foreign] media outlets about Stuxnet are efforts meant to cause concern among Iranians and people of the region and delay the launch of the Bushehr nuclear power plant."[32] Iranian president Ahmadinejad stated at a news conference that malicious software code damaged the centrifuge facilities, although he did not specifically state it was Stuxnet or the Natanz facility.[33]

Even disregarding the Siberian pipeline incident and considering Moonlight Maze the first major state-on-state cyber incident, there have been about 12 years of general practice to consider when determining what constitutes customary law in cyberspace. Incidents that have occurred during this period have set precedent for what states consider acceptable cyber behavior. What is remarkable is the lack of protest from nations whose systems have been degraded in some way by obnoxious cyber activity. Iran seemed reluctant even to admit its nuclear plant's computers had been affected and still does not claim to have been cyber attacked.[34]

If the damage caused by the Stuxnet malware had instead been caused by a traditional kinetic attack, such as a cruise missile, it is likely Iran would have vigorously responded. For one thing, in more-traditional attacks it is easier to determine the origin of attack. There are a variety of reasons Iran may have refrained from public complaint over the Stuxnet event; one possibility is that it believes the action was not prohibited under international law. Whatever the reason for Iran's silence, it remains true that no state has declared another to have violated international law by a cyber use of force or an armed attack through cyberspace. Aside from the Stuxnet event, those in Estonia and Georgia came closest.

The situation in Georgia can be distinguished because the cyber action was taken in concert with Russian troops crossing the Georgian border—a clear use of force. Cyber activity against Georgian websites did not start until after Georgia made its surprise attack on the separatist movement in South Ossetia on 7 August 2008. The cyber activity commenced later that same day, on the eve of Russia launching airplanes to bomb inside Georgian territory. It appears as though it was a military tactic to sever Georgia's ability to communicate during the attack. It was not until 9 August 2008 that Georgia declared a "state of war" for the armed attack occurring inside its territory. It did not declare the cyber activity itself an attack or use of force.[35]

A case has also been made that the 2007 massive distributed denial of service activity in Estonia was a cyber attack. However, after deliberation, even the Estonian government concluded it was a criminal act as opposed to a use of force by another state. That may be because they were not able to attribute it with certainty to the Russian government (or any other government), but the precedent remains. Attribution problems will continue to plague this area of law. It is more difficult for custom to develop if the source of the action is unknown. The actions of criminal gangs or recreational hackers do not set precedent for international law, and as long as the actor remains unknown, the events have no precedential value.

Cyber Activity and Espionage

Much of what has occurred in cyberspace between states can be viewed as merely espionage—simply intrusions onto computer systems for the collection of intelligence. If these actions are equivalent to espionage, however, this creates a dilemma in the analysis of cyber law.

Spying has been around even longer than customary international law. Despite the famous statement, "Gentlemen do not read other gentlemen's mail," espionage has existed since the earliest days of armed conflict.[36] Although the law of war addresses wartime espionage and the treatment of captured spies, customary international law is notably silent on the practice of spying during peacetime. States have domestic laws prohibiting espionage—including the United States, where spying is punishable by death—but there is no international law prohibiting espionage or insisting it violates sovereignty.[37]

Despite the absence of specific guidance, it is generally not argued that espionage is actually legal under international law. Most international lawyers contend espionage is "not illegal" internationally. Presumably, this is because it would be unseemly for countries to openly note that it is acceptable to undertake as much espionage as they can get away with. Despite the "ungentlemanly" nature of espionage, it is an open secret that countries spy on friends and foes alike. Most of the time, when spies are caught, the result is a declaration of "PNG" (persona non grata) and deportation or an exchange for other spies.[38]

The practice of nations with regard to espionage amounts to a tacit acceptance of spying. The activity is not overtly endorsed but rather occupies an ill-defined policy space that permits it to occur without violating international law. There is a general prohibition against violating territorial sovereignty, but as an exception to the rule, state practice does not prohibit spying that might involve crossing international borders without permission. Reflecting this general view, one author summarized, "The law of espionage is, therefore, unique in that it consists of a norm (territorial integrity), the violation of which may be punished by offended states, but states have persistently violated the norm, accepting the risk of sanctions if discovered."[39]

This assertion aptly illustrates the bizarre position espionage holds in the international community. Years of state practice accepting violations of territorial sovereignty for the purpose of espionage have apparently led to the establishment of an exception to traditional rules of sovereignty—a new norm seems to have been created. As cyber activities are frequently akin to espionage, even if conducted for another purpose, perhaps it is not too much of a leap to assert that most cyber activities can also occur without violating territorial sovereignty.

As states have begun to use the Internet and other computer capabilities to store, process, and communicate information, the use of cyber capabilities by intelligence agencies around the world has similarly increased. "Motives for spying [have not] changed in decades. What has changed are the means by which people spy. Cyber spying has accelerated due to increased network speeds and sophisticated chip processing capabilities."[40] One might think this would mean all nonkinetic national cyberspace operations would be governed by the loose international standards of espionage. Unfortunately, it is not quite so simple.

Manipulating cyberspace in the interest of national security began with espionage, but the continuing development of cyber capabilities means it could be used in military operations independent from espionage. Perhaps for this reason, policies and practices governing cyber espionage are more fully developed than those governing official cyber activities undertaken for other reasons. Objectively, there is little rationale for this disconnect, as most military actions in cyber would fall short of a use of force. In fact, many military actions in cyber would be indistinguishable from cyber espionage.

On the other hand, in some cases there are important differences between cyber espionage and more traditional means of spying. Surreptitiously entering a foreign country and leaving behind a sensor to collect and transmit intelligence data is one thing. But what if that sensor also contained a powerful explosive that could be detonated from a distance, causing grave destruction? If a government discovered such a device, it would be classified as a weapon of war; that would subsume any thought that it might have been placed during an espionage activity. This second scenario is perhaps more akin to some current cyber espionage techniques. Network accesses and cyber spying capabilities may be just as capable of being used for disruption of systems or deletion of data. The cyber victim may be left to wonder whether the rogue code it discovers on its network is a tool meant for espionage or attack.

A nation on the receiving end of espionage-like cyber activity (such as illicitly gaining access to a government computer network) has no sure method of discerning the intent of an intrusion and may have little notion of who is behind it. Whatever unauthorized access is gained through nefarious means could be used to collect data, destroy data, or even damage or destroy equipment. "The difference between cybercrime, cyber-espionage and cyberwar is a couple of keystrokes. The same technique that gets you in to steal money, patented blueprint information, or chemical formulas is the same technique that a nation-state would use to get in and destroy things."[41] Once illegitimate users have access to a network, they can conduct whatever mischief they like, and the software tools used by spies might well be the same as those used by criminals and saboteurs.

So, even if the target government could effectively attribute the activity to a certain state, it would not know the "why" of the activity. The nature of cyberspace does not allow for a clear distinction between intrusions for collection means and those of a more nefarious nature.

For this reason, it might follow that cyberspace operations that fall below the use of force should be covered by the same broad international law umbrella of "not illegal" that governs espionage. After all, most military cyber activities are more similar to espionage than they are to traditional military action.[42] Conceptually, there is little difference between tip-toeing into an office and stealing a sheaf of papers from a file cabinet and electronically sneaking into a computer to steal a file. There is a significant difference, however, between destroying something and a reversible action temporarily rendering something less functional. In the kinetic realm, few minimally invasive options are available. In cyber, options range from tweaking a single digit to crashing a national power grid. To treat all cyber activity equally as "attacks" is unreasonable.

To facilitate the collection of intelligence, computer code (malware) is planted in government systems. That code, in some cases, can either be used in intelligence gathering or in destructive ways, for example, to hard-break a computer system controlling e-mail at a military headquarters.

The system access created for intelligence purposes may also be used to disrupt computer systems at a level well below what would be considered a use of force under international law. Although it might be argued that the intent of the actor controls how a cyber action should be analyzed under international law, this line of argument tends to mix international and national standards of behavior.[43] A person's intent is key to many criminal charges under national law, yet in the law of war, a nation that feels threatened or as though it is under attack may not be especially concerned with the intent of the offending nation.

There is no international legal body to which states can turn to collect evidence and carefully analyze it to determine the intent behind another state's cyber activity. Neither the International Court of Justice nor other international courts can fill this role. Any evidence that existed would be classified as secret by the actor nation and would be politically sensitive as well. Witnesses would mostly be intelligence officials and politicians. In short, the system bears little resemblance to a national court system, where police officers, official reports, and witnesses may be scrutinized fully over the course of many months to determine intent. When a state becomes aware of a cyber intrusion, it must decide quickly whether it is a prelude to an attack or "merely" espionage. Even if the victim state were of a mind to inquire about intent, it might not be able to determine the source of the intrusion. Further, it might not want to disclose that it detected the intrusion.

The issue of international intent has not been much discussed as it applies under the law of war. That may be because, in the case of kinetic attacks, the intent of the attacking state is generally unambiguous.[44] This sets up an interesting conundrum. If intent does not matter in cyber operations, and only a few keystrokes determine whether a cyber activity will constitute espionage or attack, then any intrusion for collection purposes is potentially a threat or use of force. If that is the case, the UN Security Council could be set for a big increase in business.[45]

The international legal system operates under its own rules, which are established by consensus and are fundamentally different than domestic law. The law of war is driven almost entirely by the effect of actions rather than by some sort of "national mens rea."[46] The *intent* of an actor taking an action against another state that could be interpreted as hostile is, for practical purposes, irrelevant to the international law analysis.

All this leads back to the current international legal regime governing cyber activities. The question is whether state practice coincides with these norms and whether states are complying out of a sense of legal obligation. Otherwise, it is still the "Wild West" when it comes to behavior in cyberspace.

In general, cyberspace is a permissive regime, analogous to the espionage rule set—little is prohibited, but states can still do their best to prevent others from playing in the arena. There is also nothing to prevent states from prohibiting cyber behavior with national laws. Specifically, as long as cyber activity remains below the level of a use of force and does not otherwise interfere with the target nation's sovereignty, it would not be prohibited by international law, regardless of the actor's intent.

One important caveat is that aggressive cyber activities resulting in kinetic effects (i.e., physical destruction, damage, or injury) are covered by the law regarding the use of force and armed attack. They are kinetic events, governed by the traditional law of war just like kinetic effects caused by more traditional means of warfare. So, for example, a cyber event resulting in the physical destruction of a power plant turbine would be a military attack subject to the same international law governing any other kinetic attack.[47] Although determining exactly what constitutes a kinetic effect is not always simple, this line is as clear as others governing the murky corners of customary law and is clear enough effectively to distinguish cyber attacks from something less. One example of the gray area is a cyber action against an electric power grid that causes it to temporarily cease functioning. Although no actual kinetic event may occur, the reliance of modern societies on electricity for health care, communications, and the delivery of essential services makes it clear this would qualify as a kinetic-like effect and would therefore constitute a military attack if the disruption were for a significant period of time.[48]

Turning to areas of cyber operations that do not rise to the level of a military attack, there are few rules. But *few* is different than *none*, and some markers appear to have been set on the table to guide international attorneys in assessing the state of affairs.

In 2003, during the months leading up to the invasion of Iraq, the United States planned a cyber operation that would have greatly affected Iraq's financial system and frozen billions of dollars during the opening stages of the war.[49] Ultimately, US officials chose to forego this option. Reportedly, this was because they were concerned an attack on one nation's financial system would affect international confidence in the global financial system, harming the United States and its allies as well as Iraq. So, there is some question about whether they refrained due to *opinio juris* or out of mere self-interest.

In the end, it makes little difference. The financial systems of modern states are inextricably intertwined, more now than in 2003. If any nation's action would most likely damage the financial systems of many other nations, it seems this type of action would be a violation of customary international law. If for no other reason, these actions would be questionable, as they would be indiscriminate. Financial systems include banking and stock markets, essentially any "high finance" connected to the international financial system. The worldwide recession of 2007–08 demonstrated again how when one of the world's large economies sneezes, the rest are likely to catch cold.[50]

There is some potential counterevidence to this conclusion. In 2011, the NASDAQ reported an intrusion into its computer systems.[51] NASDAQ is an important financial entity, and if shut down, would certainly qualify under our definition as a cyber attack; that is, a cyber activity that is impermissible under international law. In this case, however, it appears the intrusion was detected before any harm was done, and the United States may have decided it was criminal activity not meriting a diplomatic brouhaha, or NASDAQ may have been unable to determine the source of the penetration. This does not affect the conclusion here: large-scale disruption, or destruction, of a nation's financial institutions qualifies as cyber attack.

It also appears penetration or disruption of nuclear command and control systems is a violation of customary international law. This assertion is supported by the absence of state practice to the contrary and the abundance of *opinio juris* regarding the nonproliferation and the monitoring and control of nuclear weapons.[52]

Other than these two areas, state cyber activity that falls below the level of a use of force is not prohibited under international law. It may be undertaken, just as espionage is, without sanction from the international community. Some examples of permissible behavior, as demonstrated by state practice, are penetrating and maintaining a cyber presence on government computer systems (including SCADA systems), exfiltration of government data (including the most sensitive military secrets), and denial of service or similar activities that decrease bandwidth available for government websites.

The above is premised on the thought that countries would react if they were attacked. Because all of these things have occurred but not elicited significant recriminations or a self-defense response, the conclusion is they are not attacks. However, those who take these actions in government systems run the risk of misperception that their cyber espionage is a cyber attack. If they are not armed attacks or uses of force under international law, they are not governed by the customary law of war. As a result, these disruptive cyber activities are governed by the overall customary law regime. As earlier discussed, the customary regime is permissive in the absence of norms, as is the case here. The closest existing analogy is to the rule set governing espionage. Under either the permissive or the espionage regime, disruptive cyber activities undertaken by states are permissible as a matter of customary international law, with the two exceptions (financial systems and nuclear command and control systems) noted here.

Shaping US Strategy for International Cyber Law

Because of its reliance on cyberspace, the United States should consciously craft a strategy to influence the development of customary international cyber law rather than merely observing the development. The best method to do so is through acknowledged state practice. Because of the secrecy involved in many cyberspace activities, few actually influence the development of norms. A prudent examination of US actions—and public disclosure of some—would help establish a baseline for acceptable behavior.

After the United States determines what actions it believes it is authorized to take in cyberspace, it should openly share at least examples of actions it has taken. Further, it should certainly look to the possibility of disclosing actions taken against it. By proposing certain of its own actions as acceptable and recognizing those taken against it as either acceptable or unacceptable, the United States could lead a dialogue on cyber norms, driving toward conclusions that would be beneficial for its national security.

In addition to state practice, the United States should provide releasable government materials stating what it believes are cyber norms. In May 2011 the president released the *International Strategy for Cyberspace*. This strategy recognizes that "the development of norms for state conduct in cyberspace does not require a reinvention of customary international law, nor does it render existing international norms obsolete. Long-standing international norms guiding state behavior—in times of peace and conflict—also apply in cyberspace."[53]

In recognizing that certain principles apply to cyberspace activities just as they apply to more traditional activities, the United States provides a basic framework for the cyber norms it expects will develop: upholding fundamental freedoms, respect for property, valuing privacy, protection from crime, and the right of self-defense. Although at this point, the list is more aspirational than actual, it can serve as a framework on which the United States can hang future examples of real cyber behavior by itself and others.

It is important to note that the norms set out in the *International Strategy for Cyberspace* are not universally recognized as customary international law (except for the right of self-defense). For example, although the strategy discusses fundamental freedoms such as free speech and privacy, it is apparent that particular norm is not followed worldwide. Twitter, which has been an important communications tool for government protestors in many countries, announced that it will restrict certain speech and freedom of expression if it appears to violate a local law by "reactively withhold[ing] content from users in a specific country while keeping it available to the rest of the world."[54] So, even if the United States does not, Twitter recognizes that not all these things are accepted as norms of behavior worldwide at this point.

The *Department of Defense Strategy for Operating in Cyberspace (DSOC)* recognizes the same principles and encourages the development and promotion of international cyberspace norms. The *DSOC* reiterates the *International Strategy*'s defense objective to "oppose those who would seek to disrupt networks and systems, dissuading and deterring malicious actors, and reserving the right to defend these vital national assets as necessary and appropriate."[55] Neither strategy document includes actual examples of what would be necessary and appropriate and leaves it open to interpretation. While it is helpful to provide the statement that the United States has the right to defend its vital national assets, for the purpose of customary international law it would also be helpful to know what the United States considers as a threat to those assets. On the other hand, the United States may have intentionally left this ambiguity in its international strategy to allow for the flexibility of a relevant response.

Conclusion

In the absence of formal international agreements, cyber custom is beginning to develop through the practice of states. The custom permits most cyber activity that falls below the level of a use of force, with serious actions against major financial institutions and disruptive actions to nuclear command and control systems being notable exceptions. While there has been some movement toward declarations, agreements, treaties, and international norms in the area, the hopeful statements most often heard do not coincide with current state practice. In a practical demonstration of realpolitik, states generally would like to prohibit others from undertaking the same cyber activity in which they are already engaging. The disconnect between practice and public statements creates a poor environment for negotiating international agreements and infertile soil for positive customary law—norms—to flourish. In this case, for better or worse, the default—permissive international law regime—governs. Unless states positively determine that disruptive cyber actions should be treated differently than espionage, this area will continue to be a competitive intellectual battlefield, where the cyber savvy do what they will and the cyber naïve suffer what they must.

This is not necessarily a bad-news story. Recognizing the permissive nature of cyber custom will encourage states to negotiate agreements that moderate behavior in cyberspace. To negotiate agreements, states will have to address critical cyber issues of attribution and state responsibility. In the long run, negotiated and enforceable agreements governing cyberspace may be a better option than waiting for the necessarily languid development of custom in an area that changes at the speed of thought. ⬛

Notes

1. See *Statute of the International Court of Justice*, Art. 38 (18 April 1946), http://www.icj-cij .org/documents/index.php?p1=4&p2=2&p3=0.

2. John B. Bellinger III and William J. Haynes II, "A US Government Response to the International Committee of the Red Cross Study *Customary International Humanitarian Law*," *International Review of the Red Cross* 89, no. 866 (June 2007): 443–71, http://www.icrc.org/eng /assets/files/other/irrc_866_bellinger.pdf.

3. Guidance to the contrary may be exhibited, for example, through bilateral treaties or consistent objection by other states.

4. It is a "residual negative principle which provides that in the [absence of law], whatever is not prohibited in international law is permitted." Anthea Roberts, "Traditional and Modern Approaches to Customary International Law: A Reconciliation," *American Journal of Inter-*

national Law 95 (2001): 757–91. While it is possible that the *Lotus* principle could prompt states to attempt to regulate on any matter that could affect them negatively, international law expects that states "may not exercise jurisdiction to prescribe law with respect to a person or activity having connections with another state when the exercise of such jurisdiction is unreasonable." *Restatement of the Law, Third, Foreign Relations Law of the United States*, §403, 1987 [hereinafter *Restatement*].

5. "A norm accepted and recognized by the international community of States as a whole as a norm from which no derogation is permitted and which can be modified only by a subsequent norm of general international law having the same character." *Vienna Convention on Treaties*, Art. 53, 23 May 1969, http://untreaty.un.org/ilc/texts/instruments/english/conventions/1_1_1969 .pdf.

6. The United States considers the prohibition on torture to be *jus cogens*, but as noted, the practice of nations may not support that conclusion. *Restatement*, §702, comment n.

7. *Restatement*, §102, comment b.

8. Roberts, "Traditional and Modern Approaches, 757–58.

9. *Restatement*, §102, comment c, n. 4. This comment also suggests that explicit evidence may not always be necessary to establish *opinio juris*; in some cases it may be inferred from state practice alone.

10. Peter Malanczuk, *Akehurst's Modern Introduction to International Law*, 7th rev. ed. (London: Routledge, 1997), 39.

11. Roberts, *Traditional and Modern Approaches*, 758, n. 4.

12. *Restatement*, §102, comment b.

13. See Polybius, *The Histories*, Book V, 9 (discussing the right to retaliate for sacrilegious acts committed by Aetolians), http://penelope.uchicago.edu/Thayer/E/Roman/Texts/Polybius/5* .html.

14. "The analysis of the practice of states before the conclusion of the 1967 Outer Space Treaty shows that historically, custom was the first source of the international law of outer space." Vladelen S. Vereshchetin and Gennady M. Danilenko, "Custom as a Source of International Law of Outer Space," *Journal of Space Law* 13, no. 1 (1985): 22, 25.

15. Malanczuk, *Akehurst's Modern Introduction to International* Law, 43, n. 10. See I. C. MacGibbon, "The Scope of Acquiescence in International Law," *1954 British Yearbook of International Law*, 143, 145–46; and MacGibbon, "Customary International Law and Acquiescence," *1957 British Yearbook of International Law*, 115, 138.

16. Harry Newton, *Newton's Telecom Dictionary*, 23rd ed. (New York: Flatiron Publishing, 2007), 502–3.

17. The DoD defines *cyberspace* as a war-fighting domain. Joint Publication 1-02, *DoD Dictionary of Military and Associated Terms*, 12 April 2001 (as amended through April 2010), 121.

18. As distinguished from state actions that use cyber capabilities merely as a means to accomplish a more traditional effect. For example, using e-mail to deliver a diplomatic note is legally no different than sending the note with the ambassador. The importance of "effects" is discussed below.

19. Deputy Secretary of Defense William J. Lynn III, "Remarks on Cyber," Council on Foreign Relations, 30 September 2010, http://www.defense.gov/speeches/speech.aspx?speechid=1509.

20. Bret Stephens, "Long before There Was the Stuxnet Computer Worm, There Was the 'Farewell' Spy Dossier," *Asian Wall Street Journal*, 19 January 2010, 10. In the early 1980s, a KGB officer leaked to French intelligence the names of Soviet agents involved in industrial espionage. This information was used by the West to feed misleading information to the USSR; the leaked data was referred to as the Farewell Dossier.

21. William Safire, "The Farewell Dossier," *New York Times*, 2 February 2004, http://www
.nytimes.com/2004/02/02/opinion/the-farewell-dossier.html?ref=williamsafire.

22. A denial of service (DoS) attack prevents a website from being responsive by overwhelming
it with thousands of requests (pings). Often these requests originate from a robotic network,
more commonly referred to as a botnet. "Bots" are malware-infected computers belonging to
unwitting individuals. The bots become part of a botnet—a grouping of bots—which is controlled by the unfriendly actor. Bots may be used to perform a variety of unsavory acts, such as
sending spam and collecting data for identity theft. Botnets are usually composed of computers
from many geographic locations, so the action is called a distributed DoS, or DDoS. Newton,
Newton's Telecom Dictionary, 300, n. 16.

23. A worm is a type of computer virus that can spread without human action and duplicate
itself through an entire network. A worm can allow an unauthorized user to remotely access a
computer.

24. William Ashmore, "Impact of Alleged Russia Cyber Attacks," *Baltic Security and Defence
Review* 11, no. 8 (2009).

25. Cooperative Cyber Defence Centre of Excellence (CCDCOE), *Cyber Attacks Against
Georgia: Legal Lessons Identified* (Tallinn, Estonia: CCDCOE, November 2008), 12.

26. Noah Shachtman, "Insiders Doubt 2008 Pentagon Hack Was Foreign Spy Attack," *Wired:
Danger Room*, 25 August 2010, http://www.wired.com/dangerroom/tag/operation-buckshot
-yankee/; and Sergi Shevchenko, "Agent.btz: A Threat That Hit Pentagon," *Threat Expert* blog, 30
November 2008, http://blog.threatexpert.com/2008/11/agentbtz-threat-that-hit-pentagon.html.

27. William J. Lynn III and Nicholas Thompson, "Defending a New Domain," *Foreign Affairs*
89, no. 5 (September/October 2010).

28. US Cyber Command, "Mission Statement," http://www.stratcom.mil.

29. See Google's statement at http://googleblog.blogspot.com/2010/01/new-approach-to
-china.html. Google has now resumed doing business in China.

30. Yossi Melman, "Computer Virus in Iran Actually Targeted Larger Nuclear Facility,"
Haaretz.com, 28 September 2010, http://www.haaretz.com/print-edition/news/computer-virus
-in-iran-actually-targeted-larger-nuclear-facility-1.316052.

31. Ministry of Foreign Affairs, Islamic Republic of Iran, weekly briefing, 5 October 2010,
http://www.mfa.gov.ir/cms/cms/Tehran/en/NEW/137891.html.

32. "No Delay in Launch of Bushehr Power Plant Due to Stuxnet: Official," *Tehran Times*, 5
February 2011, http://www.tehrantimes.com/index_View.asp?code=23518.

33. Mark Clayton, "Stuxnet: Ahmadinejad Admits Cyberweapon hit Iran Nuclear Program,"
Christian Science Monitor, 30 November 2010, http://www.csmonitor.com/USA/2010/1130
/Stuxnet-Ahmadinejad-admits-cyberweapon-hit-Iran-nuclear-program.

34. See, for example, Bob Sullivan, "Could Cyber Skirmish Lead U.S. to War?" *Red Tape
Chronicles*, 11 June 2010, http://redtape.msnbc.com/2010/06/imagine-this-scenario-estonia-a
-nato-member-is-cut-off-from-the-internet-by-cyber-attackers-who-besiege-the-countrys-bandw
.html; and Gary D. Brown, "Why Iran Didn't Admit Stuxnet Was an Attack," *Joint Force Quarterly*
63 (4th Quarter 2011), http://www.ndu.edu/press/why-iran-didnt-admit-stuxnet.html. In the
wake of Stuxnet, one Iranian official noted that "[a]n electronic war has been launched against
Iran," but there was never an official government statement endorsing that view. Atul Aneja,
"Under Cyber-Attack, Says Iran," *Hindu*, 26 September 2010, http://www.thehindu.com/news
/international/article797363.ece.

35. CCDCOE, *Cyber Attacks against Georgia*, 4.

36. Quoting Henry Lewis Stimson, secretary of state under Herbert Hoover, justifying closing
the "Black Chamber" in 1929, the code-breaking office. Documentation of espionage dates back

thousands of years. Egypt had an organized intelligence service 5,000 years ago, and espionage is one of the dominant themes in Sun Tzu's *Art of War* 2,500 years ago. Kurt D. Singer, *Three Thousand Years of Espionage* (New York: Books for Libraries Press, 1948), vii.

37. Some legal scholars argue that espionage is a violation of sovereignty, but this is the minority view. See Manuel R. Garcia-Mora, "Treason, Sedition and Espionage as Political Offenses under the Law of Extradition," *University of Pittsburgh Law Review* 26, no. 65 (1964): 79–80; and Quincy Wright, "Espionage and the Doctrine of Non-Intervention in Internal Affairs," in *Essays on Espionage and International Law*, ed. Roland J. Stranger (Columbus: Ohio State University Press, 1962), 12. See 18 U.S.C., pt. 1, chap. 37, "Espionage and Censorship," and 18 U.S.C., §§ 793–98, for the US domestic law.

38. For example, in July 2010 the United States and Russia exchanged spies after the FBI uncovered a Russian sleeper cell. See "U.S. Confirms Successful Exchange of Spies," *CBS News*, 9 July 2010, http://www.cbsnews.com/stories/2010/07/09/world/main6661165.shtml.

39. CDR Roger Scott, "Territorially Intrusive Intelligence Collection and International Law," *Air Force Law Review* 46 (1999): 217–18.

40. Josh Zachry, associate director for research operations, Institute for Cybersecurity, University of San Antonio, quoted in "Cyber Espionage Threatens Global Security," *Intelligencesearch.com*, http://www.intelligencesearch.com/ia158.html.

41. Tom Gjelten, "Cyber Insecurity: U.S. Struggles to Confront Threat," *NPR.org*, http://www.npr.org/templates/story/story.php?storyId=125578576.

42. See discussion of "effects" below.

43. Prescott Winter, "Cybersecurity—Governments Need to Cooperate," *Cyber Threat* blog, 8 April 2010, http://blogs.computerworlduk.com/cyber-threat/2010/04/cybersecurity--governments need-to-cooperate/index.htm#.

44. A notable exception is the case of mistake of fact or accident, such as air strikes that hit the wrong targets or targets that were unintentionally mischaracterized, in which case the victim state and the international community may assess the reasonableness of the mistake before characterizing the action under the law of war. See Daniel Williams, "NATO Missiles Hit Chinese Embassy," *Washington Post*, 8 May 1999, A-1; and "US Warplanes 'Bomb Afghan Wedding Party,'" *Independent*, 6 November 2008.

45. Art. 2(4) of the UN Charter prohibits even threats of a use of force. As states have proven themselves unwilling to give up espionage, it is unlikely the "threat of force" prohibition will be given a broad interpretation in the case of cyber activities. This might mean that states will be free under international law to implant dual-use computer code and be poised to strike, while defending states would legally be expected to wait until the moment the code was converted before acting in self-defense. A fuller discussion of this interesting issue is beyond the scope of this article.

46. *Mens rea* is a legal term referring to the intent element necessary to be convicted of a crime.

47. In a 2007 Department of Homeland Security exercise called Aurora, controlled hacking into a replica of a power plant control system enabled researchers to change the operation of a generator, resulting in its violent physical destruction. "Staged Cyber Attack Reveals Vulnerability in Power Grid," *CNN*, 26 September 2007, http://articles.cnn.com/2007-09-26/us/power .at.risk_1_generator-cyber-attack-electric-infrastructure?_s=PM:US.

48. Other factors have been suggested to form a test for a use of force. The most commonly cited is Prof. Mike Schmitt's six-part test for cyber attack, which requires assessing cyber actions for severity, immediacy, directness, invasiveness, measurability, and presumptive legitimacy. Although this is a rational test for analyzing cyber actions post facto, we would argue that only the first—severity—is necessary to determine if the event qualifies as an attack. The lightning speed

of cyber actions makes swift decision making critical, and it is unlikely nations will have the information or the time to consider these factors in the heat of potential battle. Professor Schmitt's test could be very useful in determining whether a cyber action violated an international norm not predicated on a use of force, such as the principle of nonintervention. See Michael N. Schmitt, "Computer Network Attack and the Use of Force in International Law: Thoughts on a Normative Framework," *Columbia Journal of Transnational Law* 37 (1998–99): 885; and *The Principle of Non-Intervention in Contemporary International Law: Non-Interference in a State's Internal Affairs Used to Be a Rule of International Law: Is It Still?*, Chatham House discussion group summary, http://www.chathamhouse.org.uk/files/6567_il280207.pdf.

49. John Markoff and Thom Shanker, "Halted '03 Iraq Plan Illustrates U.S. Fear of Cyberwar Risk," *New York Times*, 1 August 2009.

50. Financial Inquiry Commission, *Final Report of the National Commission of the Causes of the Financial and Economic Crisis in the United States*, January 2011, http://www.fcic.gov/report.

51. Devlin Barrett, Jenny Strasburg, and Jacob Bunge, "NASDAQ Confirms a Breach in Network," *Wall Street Journal*, 7 February 2011. For a general discussion of the National Association of Securities Dealers Automated Quotation (NASDAQ), see "NASDAQ Wiki," *Motley Fool*, http://wiki.fool.com/Nasdaq.

52. See "U.S.-Soviet/Russian Arms Control," *Arms Control Today*, June 2002, http://www.armscontrol.org/act/2002_06/factfilejune02.

53. *International Strategy for Cyberspace: Prosperity, Security in a Networked World* (Washington: White House, May 2011), 9.

54. Gerry Shih, "Twitter to Restrict User Content in Some Countries," *Reuters*, 27 January 2012, http://in.reuters.com/article/2012/01/26/twitter-idINDEE80P0IR20120126.

55. *International Strategy for Cyberspace*, 12; and *Department of Defense Strategy for Operating in Cyberspace* (Washington: DoD, July 2011), 10.